The Ultimate Meaning of
Jules De Gaultier

The Ultimate Meaning of
Jules De Gaultier

Gerald M. Spring

Philosophical Library
New York

Contents

INTRODUCTION

Jules de Gaultier's message is fundamental. What it is important to appreciate is that he understood and helped articulate the modern principle of credulity and sentimentality, our form of what he liked to designate as Bovarysm. We do indeed see life as other than it is and ourselves as other than we are.

As a relativist and an aesthete Gaultier refused to acknowledge the law of purpose as absolute and was equally averse to the domination of either faith or rationalism, which he recognized as examples of man's passion of believing. Our purpose in this book will be to demonstrate that his rejection of ethical teleology in favor of what he calls "intellectualism" does not balk human sensibility, but gives it a superior expression.

Our author was a non-typical sceptic, inasmuch as he was as concerned with building up as with tearing down. The great question, as he conceived it, was always whether or not something served the purposes of life. Thus he invariably regarded anything, that constitutes a hindrance to development or evolution, as a form of Bovarysm to attack.

We cannot stand still. In this kaleidoscope of change there can be no more than occasional glimpses or inklings of the forms of what we term real progress. What is, at all times, most needed is a well-tempered physical and a disciplined moral strength.

The Ultimate Meaning of
Jules De Gaultier

Chapter I

A Positive Philosophy
for Our Day

Chapter I

A POSITIVE PHILOSOPHY
FOR OUR DAY

THE PHILOSOPHICAL VIEW-
point presented in this work is vitalistic
and positive, as well as being in harmony
with science. The aim of life is life. Reason is seen as subservient to its purposes.

Gaultier's view of evolution, based on
the scientific writings of Quinton*, is an

* M. Quinton L'EAU DE MER MILIEU ORGAN-
IQUE, Masson, page 454.

inversion of the commonly accepted theory, which regards it chiefly as adaptation. He agrees with Quinton that it is basically an insurrection, a refusal to adapt ("un refus d'adaptation"). The principle of opposition, seen in the living biological cell and even primarily in the differentiation of object and subject, is paramount in life or existence. Evolution, it can be maintained, is a typical case of "this principle of contradiction of oneself inherent in the fact of existence." The "law of adaptation", while obviously important, is subordinate to it.

Our author repudiated what he calls "the messianism of faith", which stipulates a development from the imperfect given in diversity toward the perfection of unity. Conversely, the ideal

---

See Gaultier LA DÉPENDANCE DE LA MORALE ET L'INDÉPENDANCE DES MOEURS, pp30-34 and the chapter entitled "Une Signification Nouvelle de l'Idée d'Evolution" pp197-270. Mercure de France, Paris, 1907.

of science, which he seeks to represent, is to discover in the nature of things a universal convergence of all the diverse elements toward a unity, in which they are reconciled.

His idealistic monism, in contradistinction to dualism, makes for a joyous acceptance of life, which he interprets as "a will of representation". Its essential unity is disguised as a countless diversity. It represents the hierarchic principle and opposes "moral sensibility". Although Gaultier rejects "free will", he concedes a limited freedom. It is important to realize that his relativism, which is adjusted and corrected by experience, does not make for negativism. Throughout his work this thinker's effort is to depreciate moral sensibility in favor of a "spectacular sensibility". Perception is to be encouraged as preferable to sensation.

Gaultier regards "moral presumption", supposedly based on an alleged metaphysical objectivity, as "narrow and vain". As against this there is to be preferred the recognition of the particular compromise of each individual. The sensibility of the self and its relations with beings and things reflect affinity and repulsion and the degree of pity or of harshness demanded for its conduct by circumstances.

Certain passages in Gaultier's work are subject to possible misunderstanding. Thus the emphasis on "le refus d'obéir" (the refusal to obey) could seem inconsistent with the statement "tout ce qui vit est une chose obéissante" (Everything living is an obedient thing). Manifestly, life being creative and spontaneous, is impatient of restraint, yet undeniably the actual business of living requires and necessarily involves obedience.

Reality is seen as perfect and not susceptible of any essential change, relation and difference being its two poles. What we must endeavor to change is human reaction to it. Meanwhile phenomenal life goes on uninterruptedly with its subjective reactions of good and evil, pleasure and pain, joy and sorrow. The fact that no attempt to eliminate the undesirable factors can ever succeed should give us pause.

One of the modern sociological phenomena indicated by Gaultier is "the bovarysm of faith". The usefulness of a belief is limited to the actual power exerted on people's consciousness, to the extent that it is really believed to be true. The time has come for us to acknowledge that religious faith today has lost much of its force and is often "purely nominal".

When science is properly envisioned and its ideal understood it can make us realists and carry us beyond the stage of wishful thinking. Moral transformation, however great its apparent need, may not be our responsibility, but it is plainly our duty to recognize and point out the antinomy between the older metaphysical sensibility and our present civilization, "notre logique actuelle".

Among the most interesting and brilliant passages in Gaultier's work are the discussions of justice.* He considers it contradictory to conceive an absolute of perfection, which has not always been such. Among his commentaries one finds the statement "the two ideas of being and becoming exclude each other". Evolution from one state to another implies time, which is not accounted for in the

---

* For example in LA SENSIBILITÉ MÉTA-PHYSIQUE and in COMMENT NAISSENT LES DOGMES.
See in the first the passage on page 55. Note also in LA DÉPENDANCE DE LA MORALE ET L'INDÉPENDANCE DES MOEURS, page 335.

idea of the absolute being. "The fact that the world is given in becoming and relation implies that its true nature is that of becoming and relation". "How", he queries, "is one to reconcile with the idea of justice essential to the moral ideal, present and past imperfection, the contrast of completed epochs given over to pain and evil with the blissful serenity of the day after tomorrow?" Surely the past is a part of the whole, which is the object of metaphysics.

According to the author justice is "a form of the feeling of power objectifying the modalities characteristic of an individual sensibility in the universal". Although founded on sympathy it is not too much to say that, in practice, what is called "just" is no more than a specific instance of "the unjust".

In his view ethics does not, of itself, admit of justification, inasmuch as imperfection, the medley of pain and pleasure, is the condition of existence. The messianic ideal, whose essence is indefinite hope, is the source of movement, the means of change. Aesthetic activity, on the other hand, is expressed in a kind of contemplation, which immediately enjoys its object. In fact Gaultier designates his aesthetic sense as "a second form of sensation, in which it justifies itself."

One cannot but admire a realistic thinker, who recognizes the universality of injustice in a sensible way. It does not deter him nor prevent him from developing his very positive aesthetic and spectacular philosophy. There are indubitably some analogies to Nietzsche's thought, but the philosophy of Jules de Gaultier is grounded on his conception, original with him, termed Bovarysm. Fundamentally it is a difference in emphasis, notwithstanding the agreement of the two authors in many things.

He called attention to two possibilities, one a development in the direction of culture and the other toward universal well-being. Clearly it is the former that he considers favorable to life and hence preferable. It will become ever clearer, as we proceed in the study of this French thinker, that modern sociology partakes too much of the nature of a religion to warrant its being considered a science.

We must understand what, for Gaultier, would be progress. He wishes perception to be developed *more* in relation to sensation and this is a matter of discipline and helpful to culture.

Here there is a temptation, rightly or wrongly, to envision such a possibility as something that Nietzsche would have approved. Could one not perhaps regard a development of this sort as something in the nature of a partial realization of his ideal of the superman?

Chapter II

Spiritualism
Without Theology

Chapter II

SPIRITUALISM
WITHOUT THEOLOGY

N THE PROCESS OF FAMILIAR-
izing himself with the writings of Jules de
Gaultier a neophyte could think and be
inclined to sustain the impression that he
was dealing with one of the more dis-
cerning French intellectuals and go no
further. That he is, indeed, an interesting
and original thinker is undeniable, but

27

let us try to avoid an inadequate appraisal. It will become clear, as we continue,
that his importance lies mostly in another challenge. Gaultier was an innova-
tor, whose philosophy involves the whole
man and requires more than the critical
intellect. Nothing is more central in his
thought than his desire that one forgo
moral sensibility in favor of a "metaphysical sensibility", the meaning of which
we hope to clarify.

The author defines reality ("le réel") as
"a fact of opposition between two states
of one and the same force" and specifies
that "this opposition arises, in a form of
conflict, between a power of impulsion,
creating movement, outside of which no
reality is conceivable, and a power of arrest, which, slowing down the flux of this
original movement according to a thou-
sand nuances, sculptures the forms of the
phenomenon at the will of an infinity of

diverse combinations." What is supposed to be essential in the theory is "the fact of opposition itself, that a force be divided with itself", causing self-contradiction and antagonism "in order that the life of relation, the real may come into being."

Gaultier seems in fundamental agreement with Nietzsche as to culture, which implies a fact of repetition, representing the power of arrest, "the apollinic sense which, amid the monstrous effusion of dionysiac exuberance, introduces lines and contours", invoking the forms of reality. He calls attention to the fact that Nietzsche contradicts himself when he celebrates by turns the superman and culture. Therein, Gaultier insists, the German thinker is only imitating life, which is essentially contradiction rather than logic.

Sociology, which he calls "the new idol" is not the science as which it has been represented, but the modern successor to theology. Reason continues to be secondary and cannot thwart the major purposes of life. In biology, which treats of living organisms, there is not only an extraordinary diversity, but a differentiation between superior and inferior. In our author we have a modern thinker, who is wary of general ideas and disposed to warn us against being duped by them. Nothing, he contends, is more needed than a positive acceptance of reality *as it is,* according to the way in which it is experienced.

Gaultier considers the Christian idea to be the most universal expression of the principle or law of participation. In order to understand this "law of participation", which he expounds in LA SENSIBILITÉ MÉTAPHYSIQUE, one must consider the mystical character of "collective representations", all of which, in varying forms and in varying degrees, imply a "participation between beings and objects linked in a collective representation". The author refers us to a work by Lévy-Bruhl * and the definition given by that writer. He finds the tragedy of our epoch in the attachment of our conservatives to certain "traditional fictions", which prevent the appreciation of the reality of civilization. He inveighs with great eloquence against the "chimerical ideology", which we owe to our desire for perfection, happiness and equality.

Inasmuch as Christianity today is less otherwordly, it tends to stress the satisfaction of the most immediate appetites, so that inferior instincts like cupidity and

*Lucien Lévy-Bruhl LES FONCTIONS MENTALES DANS LES SOCIÉTÉS INFÉRIEURES. Félix Alcan, Paris, 1910.
See Gaultier LA SENSIBILITÉ MÉTAPHYSIQUE, pp 52-53 and the chapter "Une Signification Nouvelle de l'Idée d'Évolution" in LA DÉPENDANCE DE LA MORALE ET L'INDÉPENDANCE DES MOEURS.

envy are encouraged. The brakes of dogma prove to be of little avail and at a time of lessened faith, with the present force of an equalitarian ideology, the proletarian masses inevitably have their innings. Gaultier sees this development as very dangerous and a. potentially catastrophic for our world.

Our author did not shrink from recognizing and exposing weaknesses in modern man's religious pretensions, but his philosophy does treat of the whole man and is not neglectful of his emotional needs. The title of one of his later works LA VIE MYSTIQUE DE LA NATURE can give a hint of this.

As a relativist Gaultier, no less than Nietzsche, combatted the idea of Good in itself. He points out how man, unable to separate the idea of morality from that of happiness, tends to see the former as "a sagacious means of attaining felicity". Indeed, how rationalism takes the place of theology and pursues the same task "in a more direct manner" is developed in his book NIETZSCHE ET LA RÉFORME PHILOSOPHIQUE.* ". . . .with the idea of Good in itself, the metaphysical spirit, interpreter of popular passion, made the most violent effort to counteract force with a principle, which would be superior to it and furnish morality with an immutable basis."

Both faith and rationalism desire certainty. In either case men are dominated by the passion to believe, by the need for a fixed truth permitting them to dispense with further intellectual effort. Intellectualism in the philosophical sense is opposed to both. What is involved in intellectualism, Gaultier maintains, is the entirely different need to employ the activity of mind, this exercise bringing

* See the chapter entitled "Le Parti Pris Sociologique" in NIETZSCHE ET LA RÉFORME PHILOSO-PHIQUE, Mercure de France, Paris, 1905.

with it complete satisfaction. It has nothing to do with any reactions of one's sensibility, like pleasures or deceptions, to the propositions. It is, in his view, a question of achieving an ever more ample coherent system of reality, by the extent of which our mental powers are measured.

In case the author's strictures of "moral sensibility" raised some eyebrows, the reader should remember how unequivocally he stated the necessity of obedience for life in any form.

There are distinct forms of psychic energy. The passage elaborating this certainly proves the consistency of the philosopher in his idealistic monism.** One comes from the belief in the reality of the external world and it is under the

** See LA VIE MYSTIQUE DE LA NATURE, Chapter II, especially pp26-29. Éditions Crès et Compagnie, Paris, 1924. Also COMMENT NAISSENT LES DOGMES, pp 245-248. Mecure de France, Paris, 1912.

sway of this belief that the psychic activity seeks to possess the objects of this world. It strives to understand its laws and is determined to bring everything under its domination. By manifold analyses it applies itself to reducing it to its primary elements. The activity of the second sort, on the other hand, regards the belief in the independent reality of the world of objects as illusory. It takes a mystical form bent on dispelling the "hallucination" by progressively reducing "the difference between the psychic energy itself and the objects of the external world, in which it is reflected, in terms of which it takes cognizance of itself."

Gaultier blames philosophical impotence on two factors, a sentimental error and an intellectual error. The first, pertaining to the moral conception, seems the more fundamental one to him, although it could not have come about without the other. The intellectual error is one of realism, having to do with attributing an objective entity to time, space and matter, thus making the moral conception of existence feasible. "It became possible to conceive in the universe, after having introduced it into it, an activity distinct from that of thought". The famous German metaphysician, Immanuel Kant, deals with this so-called "noumenal reality", which he declared to be inaccessible to us.

Of the two modes of seeing reality the author prefers the second or mystical one. He seeks to demonstrate how the passage from transcendence to immanence has not made too fundamental a change in human sensibility. Human beings differ from animals in that they have lost the faculty of living in the instant. If they ignore the immediate interest of the present, it is because they do not even perceive it. What Gaultier blames for this is "the illusion of finalism". He explicitly repudiates the law of purpose or what is denominated "final cause".* The desired passage from a religious to a lay conception has been hindered and prevented by what he designates as an "immanent messianism".

* We refer the reader to the interesting and eloquent passage in Gaultier's LA SENSIBILITÉ MÉTAPHY-SIQUE, pp 48-49.

Chapter III

The Significance
of Élitism

Chapter III

THE SIGNIFICANCE OF ÉLITISM

THE CONCEPT OF EQUALITY has come to play such an important rôle in modern sociology that its intellectual nature tends to be forgotten. As a consequence we neglect hierarchy, the more fundamental principle in life and biology. Realism requires that this again be more stressed.

41

Authors, who favor élites, are prone to write passages that are definitely anti-Christian. Should we, then, consider abandoning the values that we associate with Christian civilization? By no means, for values are values. But where weakness has been encouraged in the practice of the Christian religion, there must be a reappraisal and a different interpretation of this ideal. The mistakes, which have been made, are due to a form of bovarysm.

That Gaultier, no less than Nietzsche, appreciated and greatly valued the idea of hierarchy one gathers from his two works on that German thinker, an earlier book NIETZSCHE ET LA RÉFORME PHILOSOPHIQUE and a later one entitled NIETZSCHE. We owe to Gaultier some interesting evaluations of Frederick Nietzsche's work. Thus, referring to THE WILL TO POWER, he speaks of "the divine enterprise" attempted by the German philosopher in seeking to "replace the hypothesis of causality by that of a conflict in which, at every moment, all the forces of existence are engaged and render their final consequences." Moreover, he points out that in THUS SPAKE ZARATHUSTRA he has ZARATHUSTRA say: "Of Hazard—that is the oldest nobility in the world; that gave I back to all things; I emancipated them from bondage under purpose."

Gaultier refers to a passage in BEYOND GOOD AND EVIL, one in which Nietzsche made clear that he considered exploitation to be "the natural consequence of the will to power", belonging, he maintained, "to the essence of life as a fundamental organic function." Tyranny and exploitation are words that men decry, but let us remember that we human beings are a part of biology. Gaultier saw us as subject to the general laws of evolution. He called attention to it being "a fact of caesarism" that brought about the first organism.

Our author admired Nietzsche for his partiality toward "ascending life" and his willingness to accept the means of realizing it. This means that, like the German thinker, he favored aristocracy, since the fact of supremacy, based on force, presides at every evolution in such a direction. He too sees the élite as the principle of change and the mass as the principle of immobility, of stability. While conceding the necessity of arrest having a rôle in producing social reality, he contemns its excess.*

Life is lived by means of fictions. In his discussion of Nietzsche Gaultier brings out that the will to truth is itself but "a feint of the will to power, some Trojan horse, some ruse to prevail."

* See LE BOVARYSME, édition du Mercure de France, page 304.
BOVARYSM, Philosophical Library, New York, 1970. (Page 170)

44

The Christian idea should never be allowed to become a shield for the weak. In approving the strong and promoting strength it is obvious that certain considerations must always predominate. What counts is what is best for the individual, for the family and for the social group, the nature of what is best being determined by experience.

Gaultier traces Christian sensibility and morality to Socrates and to Plato, who "mounted the tripod" and spoke like an oracle. It is to him and his vaticinations that we owe the phantoms of ideas, which were abstracted from the rich and concrete world of experience and, consequently, the creation of a "humanitarian section". He shows us that, as a result, an *ideological* realism tended to replace an *idealistic* nominalism.

In his philosophy Jules de Gaultier seems to be entirely in accord with Nietzsche's view of the Roman Catholic

Church. Here again it is a question of appreciating hierarchy. Thus he refers to the "pagan atmosphere reconstituted in Rome by the catholicism of the popes" and avers that its implicit submission to the aspirations of the mass ("le nombre") is more apparent than real. It is well-known that the German philosopher classed Catholicism, the Renaissance and humanism among anti-Christian phenomena. Our author shows how, by virtue of its dogma, the most dangerous principles of Christianity were turned to account so as to benefit social values. Only when dogma is relaxed, as under the influence of The Reform, have we any reason to apprehend a danger from those "deadly principles".*

The rationalistic conceptions of ab-

* This, written from the Catholic point of view, is interesting and understandable, although no one of a Protestant tradition or persuasion would be likely to agree entirely with such an appraisal.

solute good, absolute justice and universal equality do not correspond to the conditions of phenomenal life. We owe this bovarysm to Karl Marx and socialism, because of kinds and degrees of injustice, that had become intolerable in his day. That some good was originally achieved must be granted, but we have now come full circle, having reached the extreme of a fanatical egalitarianism, from which no further benefits can be expected.

Modern life, as we know it, manifests some disorder, since there is enough of a revolutionary psychology to make for disruptions and vandalism. We must rid ourselves of hate and envy in order, once again, to achieve cooperation and a positive spirit involving a respect for order.

Not only is hierarchy, in a sense, inevitable, but rightly understood it should become a social ideal and be regarded as the essence of the modern state. The idea of service accords with it quite as well as with the Christian ideal. Everyone serves something or someone in a hierarchy. Have we not had enough, of pride and arrogance? There has been too much loose talk about slavery and one tends to forget slavery to weakness and to vice in different forms. All must be dedicated to the good of the whole. If there is to be a race of masters, it should be recognized that these are, in their turn, servants. Those endowed with the privilege of wisdom or of wealth should be expected to give of what they have for social needs.

What is most fundamental in Gaultier's point of view is the substitution of the idea of "a natural reality" for the theological conception of reality. He traces what he calls "rationalistic sensibility" to Kant and Rousseau, both of whom conceived an idea of "the good" as an objective reality.

Our author's positive and empirical

conception of "the real" differs from the theological view in its consistent monism. "The same living energy, which creates the real in the course of and amidst the avatars of an aleatory evolution, simultaneously creates the law of this reality.** He therefore rejects the imposition on the living energy of a finality representing an aim external to itself and immutable.

** Jules de Gaultier LA DÉPENDANCE DE LA MORALE ET L'INDÉPENDANCE DES MOEURS, page 116.

Chapter IV

The Spectacular
Philosophy

Chapter IV

THE SPECTACULAR
PHILOSOPHY

A VERY FUNDAMENTAL WORK
of Jules de Gaultier's, one of his later ones,
is LA SENSIBILITÉ MÉTAPHYS-
IQUE *, in which his purpose is to oppose
an aesthetic sensibility to a moral sensibility. It represents an eloquent and

* LA SENSIBILITÉ MÉTAPHYSIQUE, Editions du
Siècle, Paris, 1924.

cogent attack on what he calls "moral messianism". On page thirteen we find the following passage: "Founded on sensation, on the unique consideration of joy and of suffering, this messianic conception of a world evolving from evil and imperfection toward the perfection of the Good aims at nothing less than realizing joy by eliminating suffering, that is to say outside of the relation, which engenders it, outside of the conditions determining it." The author points out how such a logical contradiction inevitably led to a moral pessimism.

Gaultier himself has told us that life is contradiction. What he here attempts seems like the impossible, since his aim is to change human psychology in this regard. His monistic conception of the world as a "will of representation" is very interesting. It must be left to the reader to what extent he judges this thinker to have been successful in his certainly laudable aim.

Our author likes to think of philosophers as artists, as "artistes du réel", namely of reality in the way we know it. Owing to the "principle of movement" reality is, of course, constantly changing, but what we have to recognize is the necessity of accepting reality as it is, inasmuch as it is not susceptible of any fundamental change. This Gaultier does and more. He calls it beautiful and perfect and glories in it. In this fact we have a remarkable change in viewpoint, which is potentially of great significance.

Gaultier prizes the aesthetic sense, to which biology has slowly attained at the summit of its evolution, because it is the means for the mind "to distinguish in reality this perfection which is essential to it."

The "chimerical conception" of moral messianism is thus easily discarded in favor of a philosophy consistent with the idea of life or existence being "a will of representation".

Concerning the spectacular point of view, which we owe to the idealistic axiom conditioning existence through the knowledge of self, it may be said that "it constitutes expressly a metaphysics of the phenomenon." This idealism the author not only considers compatible with strict intellectualism, but he sees it as the source of "the most positive views". His phenomenalism implies the relativity of every phenomenon and the relativity of all knowledge.

The reader could not have failed to note our author's remarkable concurrence with Frederick Nietzsche, whom he transcends in certain ways. Where Gaultier definitely agrees with the German thinker is in his opposition to "the democratic ideal", the "Christian-equality" doctrine, which in his view represents a danger to Western civilization. But, while equally sensible of the meaning of power and the part it plays in life, he differs from that philosopher in his emphasis on aesthetics.*

Moreover, he shows humility and reverence, which is unusual in a modern, who is trained in science and beyond the stance of the old-fashioned believer. Religion not only was, but is and always will be creative. It would seem the fact of understanding that one is, ineluctably, a myth-maker, helps one to be tolerant. We hope to be able to show that Gaultier comes closer than Nietzsche to giving moderns a faith.

Gaultier's interest in and tolerance of

* See, in this connection, the interesting and important monograph by Wilmot E. Ellis entitled BOVARYSM. THE ART PHILOSOPHY OF JULES DE GAULTIER, which contains a translation of the French author's autobiographical notes. Number Sixteen, University of Washington Chapbooks, edited by Glenn Hughes. Seattle, Washington 1928.

Highly recommended is a book by a compatriot: LA PHILOSOPHIE DU BOVARYSME by Georges Palante, Mercure de France, Paris, 1912. This book also has a portrait of the author and an autograph.

religion is necessarily limited to such forms as prove consistent with his intellectual outlook. He calls attention to the fact that theological conceptions explain the world by a principle, which is external to it. One has really said nothing by explaining the world by the divine, since the divine itself remains to be explained. Furthermore, when we come to the rationalistic philosophy, we find that it is a substitution of ideology for theology, inasmuch as the notion of the law or the idea replaces that of God.* As for science and the theory of evolution men came to "imagine a selection holding sway in the moral world as it had in the physical world." Consequently they tended to believe in finality or teleology, the law of purpose.

Our author regards the viewpoint of

* See Jules de Gaultier LA SENSIBILITÉ MÉTAPHYSIQUE, pages 42-49.

unity in the absolute, which slights
diversity in relation, as fundamentally
pessimistic, as an "aspiration to nothing-
ness". One cannot but congratulate him
on his rejection of the extraneous principle and the viewpoint so long favored by
moral philosophy. Gaultier was one of
the Western thinkers most fruitfully in-
fluenced by Oriental philosophy. The
meaning that Buddhistic pantheism had
for him may be gathered from a passage
in his autobiographical notes. Appar-
ently it was Arthur Schopenhauer, who
was responsible for his initiation into the
hindouistic and pantheistic view of the
world.**

We are dealing with a philosophy,
which is rigorously monistic. His
idealism insists that the fact of relation
conditioning reality results from a "fact

** See the above-mentioned work by Wilmot E. Ellis
on Bovarysm, pages 36-38.

of opposition" exemplifying "the principle of contradiction". Our author regards time, space and causality as "means of representation". As we know, he deprecates the idea of there being an evolution from a state of imperfection toward one of perfection. Moralists would fain see happiness equally distributed among all individuals, but the aim springing from such a solicitude is never attained. With this concern "I engender movement" and do no more than "change the landscape of the universe".***

Therefore Gaultier favors "the substitution of perception for sensation as center of interest, as the essential activity of existence. . . ." He makes the point that sensation, even when painful, is justified, if one can see in it a means of

*** Jules de Gaultier LES RAISONS DE L'IDÉALISME, Introduction, pages 20-21.

perception. He has defined existence as a
"phenomenon of thought". From the
point of view of his monistic idealism the
belief in the reality of the external world
is the fundamental delusion ("men-
songe") or "the essential Bovarysm, on
which reposes the existence of thought".
In his philosophy, then, phenomenalism
replaces "the disappointing conception
of Kantian illusionism".*

Our author naturally repudiates the
view of the realists, who regard phenomena as "illusory". In his opinion they
"confound the modes of production of
the phenomenon with laws", which, they
think, could allow one to attain to a
"noumenal objectivity". As against the
realism of sensation, one of moral sensibility, which is also a realism of space
and time, the spectacular sensibility

* See Georges Palante LA PHILOSOPHIE DU
BOVARYSME, especially pages 44 and 45.

recommended by him implies "a strictly relativistic conception of the real".

Gaultier regarded Julian Benda as "un philosophe spectaculaire". There is an intellectual affinity between him and Benda, the author of *La Trahison des Clercs* and BELPHÉGOR. Both were averse to Bergson's intuitionism and his views on aesthetics.**

The point of view we are considering is a substitution of aesthetics for ethics, an attempt at what could be designated as a visual philosophy. We are to see certain antonyms or contrasts like good and evil, pain and pleasure, beauty and ugliness as in a picture. Moreover the author counsels us to transform our emotions into landscapes.

As Gaultier sees it, there are two "genres" or modes of which he favors the

** See Gaultier's essay *Le Réalisme du Continu* in Revue Philosophique, Félix Alcan, Paris, 1910. (Interesting discussions of Plato, Kant and Bergson)

second or mystical one, which leads one to disbelieve the reality of external objects: "The sentiment of nature is one of the creations of this second genre, which is of a mystical order and finds its ultimate expression in ecstasy".***

*** This passage occurs in Gaultier's LA VIE MYS-TIQUE DE LA NATURE on page 28.

Conclusion

Conclusion

ACCORDING TO GAULTIER THE irrational must be seen as predominant, as that from which everything including what one calls "reason", flows: "L'Irrationnel est au principe de la raison". If indeed, as he alleges, error is the true source of knowledge, it would be well to remember this in our mental improvisation. The power to imagine, even to conceive, is essentially creative. Let us, then, endeavor to make the most intelligent use of the principle of bovarysm and be guided by experience.

We seem to be in what has been called an "Integrity Crisis". Manifestly there is today a failure to recognize or fully appreciate the importance of certain essentials of social reality. In fact, as some have pointed out, we are facing as one of our crucial problems "a massive loss of confidence in law".

In these days there appears to be little if any respect for authority. As an unfortunate and inevitable consequence we are traversing a period marked by disorder as evidenced by unparalleled crime and vandalism.

There are those, who would blame this social breakdown on the fact that science has tended to replace religion. Such an interpretation of a complex matter is hardly admissible, although we are certainly in a scientific age.

We have said that our author is not religious and he is not in any theological sense, but he is more than a scientist and intellectual. He is an intelligent mystic and in his monism and his aesthetic philosophy we have something like a challenge, which could satisfy man's emotional needs. His is a positive philosophy furthering a joyful response to life. It is not too much to say that Gaultier is a great soul and that he fulfills a need at this moment in time.